RYCO and RONEKA TAYLOR

My Journey as a Preemie Baby

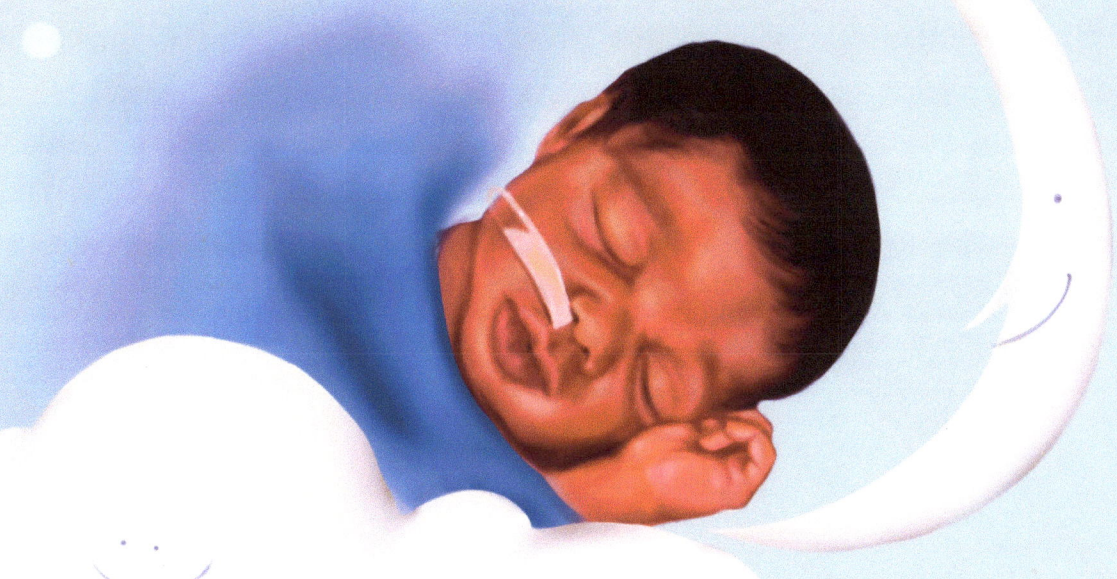

Illustrated by Elena Lisovskaya

My Journey as a Preemie Baby
Copyright © 2023 by Ryco and Roneka Taylor.

Illustrations Copyright Property of Ryco and Roneka Taylor.

All rights reserved. No part of this book may be reproduced or transmitted in any form or by any means without written permission from the author/publisher.

Published in the United States

ISBN 9781088169919

I wrote this book about my journey as a preemie baby because I am grateful to still be here to grow and play with my friends. Life is fun. This book is dedicated to my family, friends, and premature babies everywhere.
I hope you enjoy it!

-Ryco L. Taylor

The doctor told Mommy she couldn't have any more babies, but she was wrong.

Mommy was scared when she found out she was pregnant with me because she was taking medicine for her cancer not to come back.

The doctor calmed Mommy down and told her to go take a test to make sure the cancer medicine didn't hurt me.

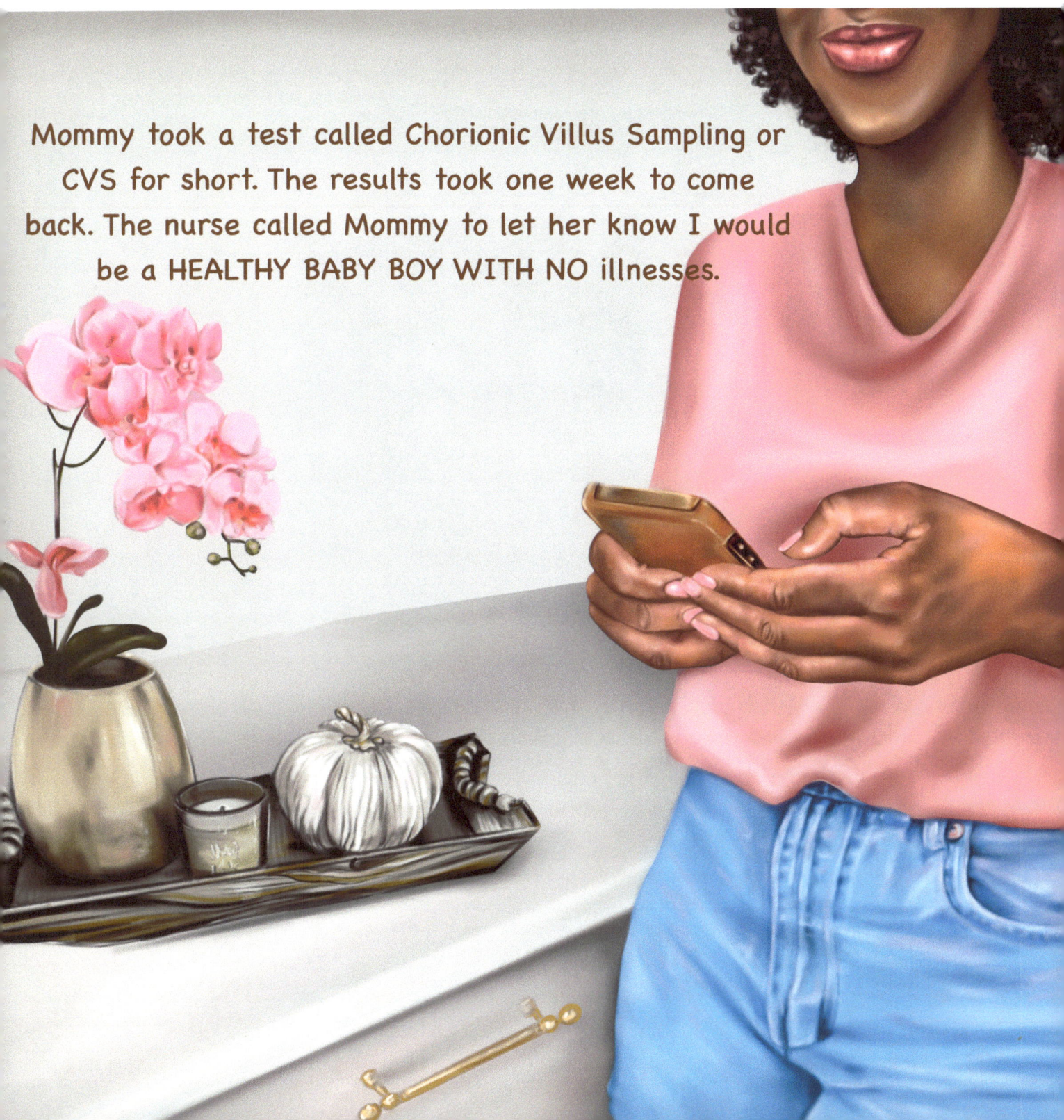

Mommy took a test called Chorionic Villus Sampling or CVS for short. The results took one week to come back. The nurse called Mommy to let her know I would be a HEALTHY BABY BOY WITH NO illnesses.

Mommy was sad and cried a lot when she was pregnant with me.

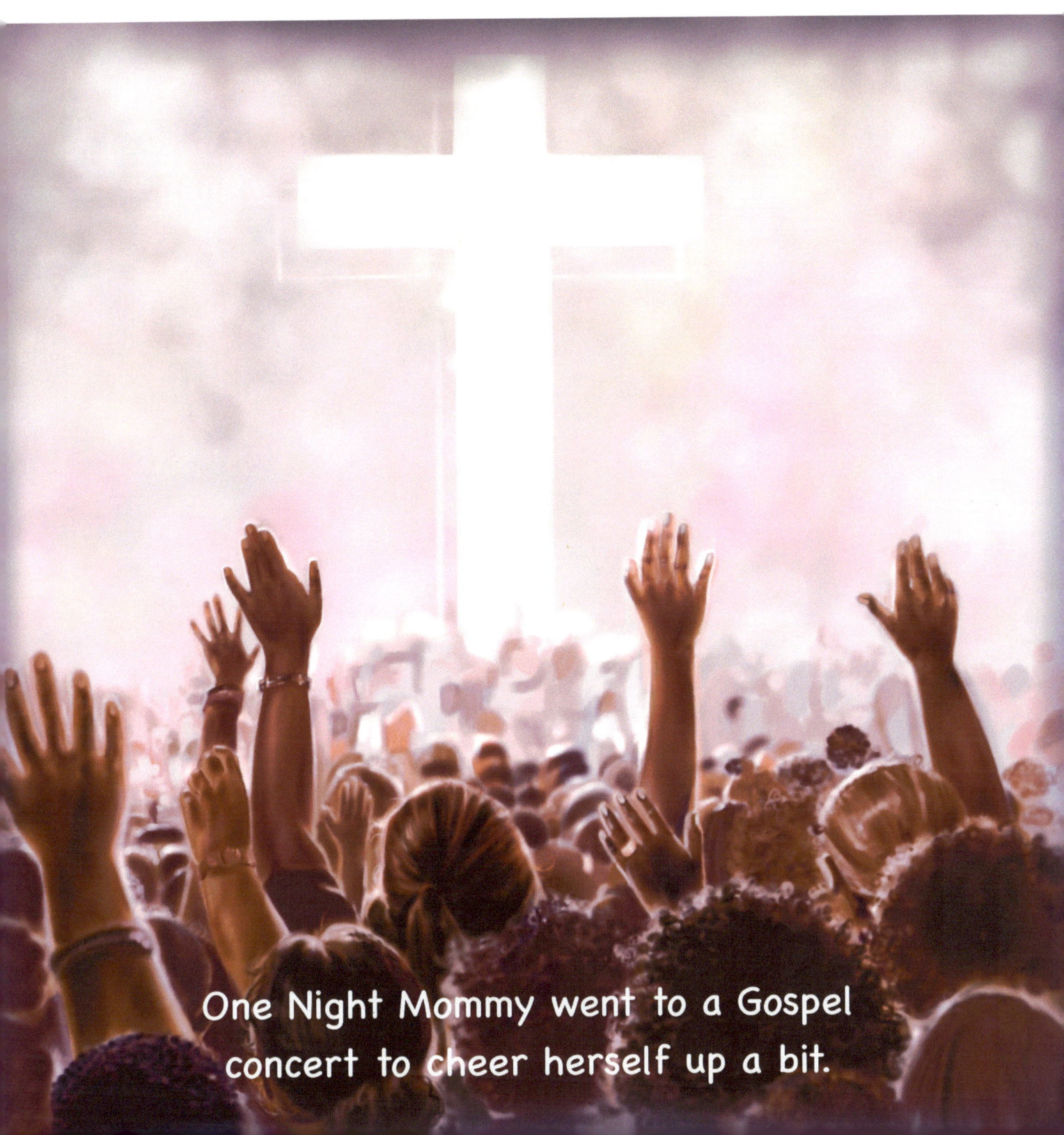
One Night Mommy went to a Gospel concert to cheer herself up a bit.

Mommy called the hospital and the nurse told her to get to the Emergency room at Long Beach Memorial hospital as soon as possible.

Mommy found out she had to spend a few nights at the hospital for them to watch me closely.

A few days later the doctors were worried because they couldn't hear my heartbeat. They told Mommy she had to have an emergency caesarean to save me.

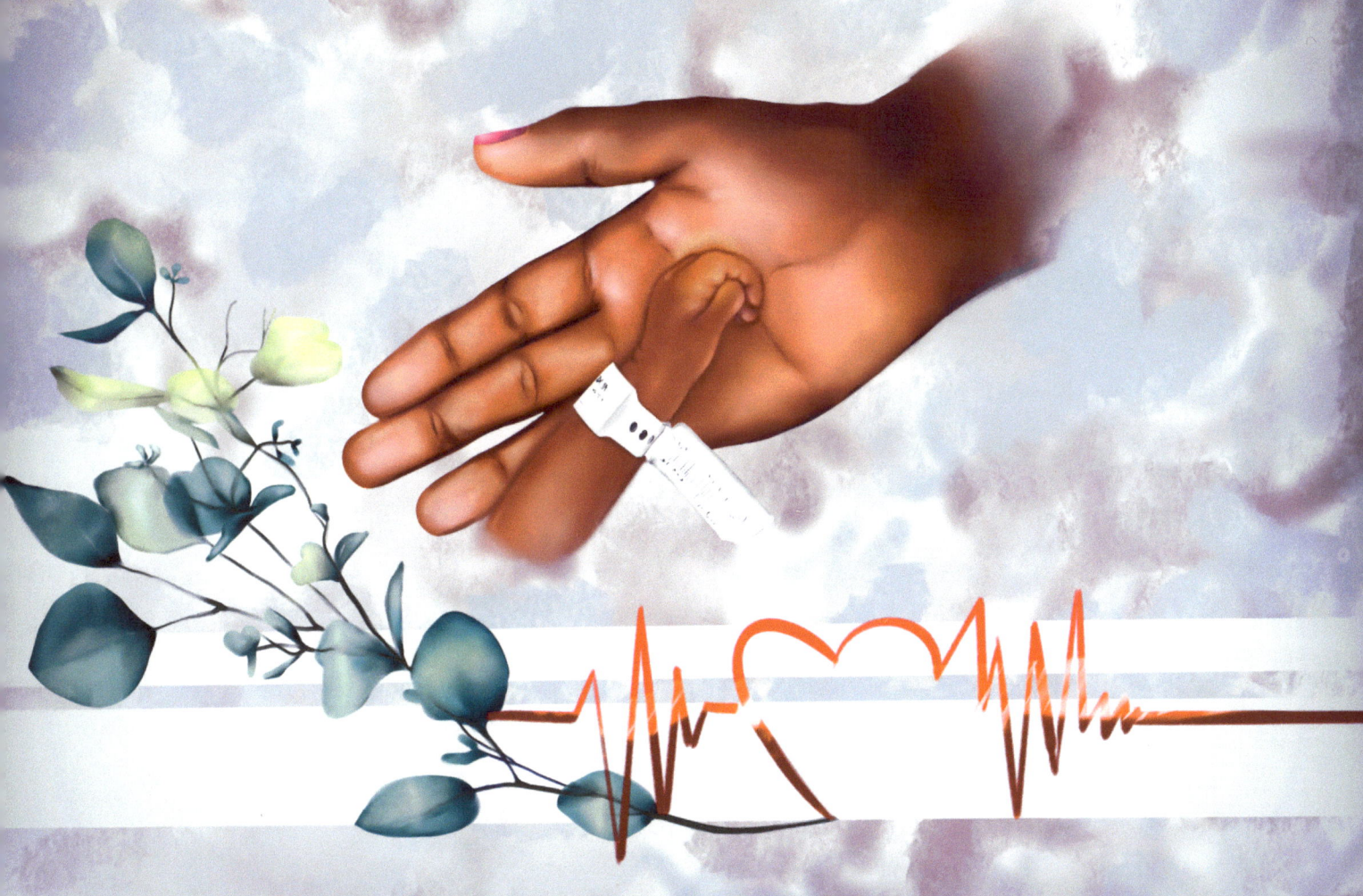

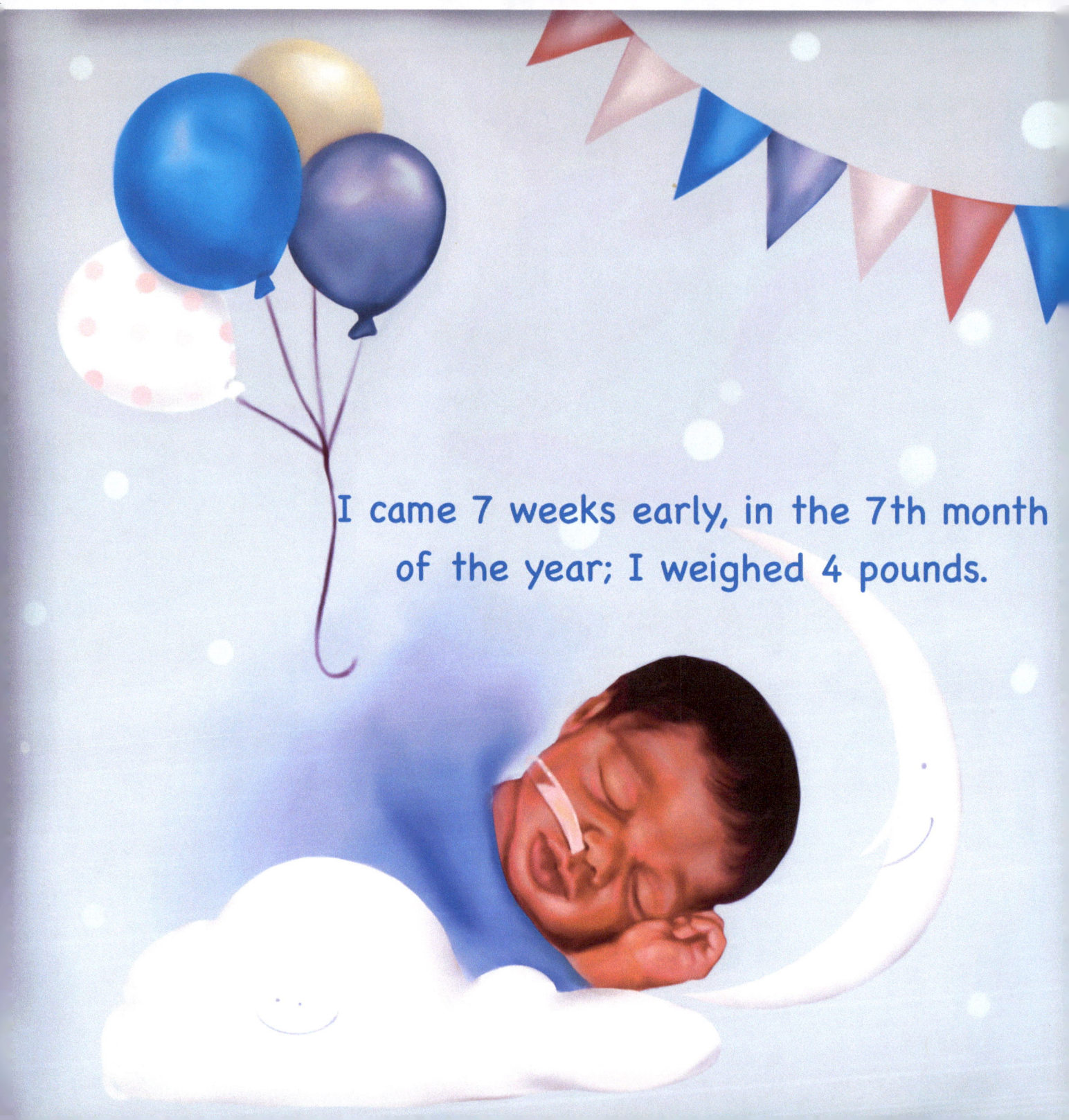

I had to spend a month in Neonatal Intensive Care Unit (NICU) because I couldn't eat, had tubes everywhere, and was too little to go home. Mommy prayed every day I was there. She also visited me all day every day to make sure I knew she loved me.

Mommy couldn't feed me her milk because of her breast surgeries and that made her sad.

Everyone everywhere prayed for me, and God healed me and helped me grow.

Yo hablo español

Now I am OK and big and smart. I'm learning Spanish, soccer, and how to be an amazing Artist.

My big sister Cortney taught me how to draw, takes me to the park, and always plays with me.

One day I was talking to my big sister Coryn, and she told me she was Mommy's favorite. I said, "But I'm Mommy's MIRACLE!"

Preemies are God's miracles. It does not matter how small you start, as long as you have a big heart.

Printed in the USA
CPSIA information can be obtained
at www.ICGtesting.com
LVHW080353011023
759757LV00008B/154